Feel Good Factor in 30 Days

Andrea Morrison

Eden House Publishing

Copyright © Andrea Morrison 2014

First Published 2014

All rights reserved. Without limiting the rights under copyright reserved above, no part of this publication may be reproduced, stored in or introduced into a retrieval system or transmitted, in any form or by any means (electronic, mechanical, photocopying, recording or otherwise) without the prior written permission of both the copyright owner and the above publisher of this book.

www.edenhousepublishing.com

The author of this book does not prescribe the use of any techniques in this book as a form of medical advice or treatment or substitute thereof without the advice of a general practitioner or physician.

The intent of the author is to provide information of a general nature only to help you in your journey towards seeking happiness and wellbeing in your life.

In the event that you do use any of the information in this book for yourself you do so at your own risk.

Dedication

This book is dedicated to my wonderful, long suffering and ever patient husband Paul, who has really stuck by me over the last twenty years and has always believed in me no matter what and who has given me the most beautiful three children.

Life is definitely a journey, and we've had a great one!

Andrea Morrison - My Story

My journey started many, many years ago. I left school with mediocre qualifications and obtained a training contract with the local government, but I had a dream – a big dream. I had always wanted to be a Barrister since I was in junior school – but had been told by various teachers that 'people like me do not do jobs like that' and the schools I had attended were failing schools.

Then I met a kindred spirit! My husband wanted to travel, to do something different with our lives – so we combined it! After travelling around Europe and America, we back packed around South America and I went back to University to pursue my dream. I had already become successful in Local Authority and Durham University was quick to snap me up!

Fast forward several years and I really had it all. I was a Barrister in a fantastic local Chambers, I was Treasury Counsel appointed by the Attorney General, I had been led by a top employment QC, I was even in the Legal 500 – I was living my dream with a brilliant career ahead of me or so you might think. But something had dramatically changed in my life, I'd started a family, a family that I had desperately wanted and had battled through infertility to get – suddenly working ridiculous hours and travelling the length and breadth of the country was soul destroying, handing over my children to (an amazing) childminder quite frankly broke my heart. Also during this time, my Father had died of cancer, he was a big influence in my life and then he was gone, it made me think about the fragility and shortness of life. I knew in ten years time, my children would be grown up and my relationship with them fragile if not nonexistent.

During 2008, after my third child, even though I was at my lowest ebb I gave it my all in my belief that if I did it I could finally balance it all. Be the mum I wanted to be and the Barrister I knew that I was – and create the home my family deserved (yes we embarked on a two storey extension to our home!). But of course life isn't like that, and I wasn't superwoman and in November 2008 I ended up with pneumonia. I simply had burnt myself out.

It may be difficult to believe, but it was not a personal drive to be a 'career women' but a belief that I *should* be a career woman, to do anything else was a failure, a waste, that I was letting my family down both financially and emotionally. I had to carry on, to simply put my children first and be predominantly at home was simply not an option.

I stumbled through the following year, our marriage was facing a major crisis, a holiday finally highlighted to us that we were trying to do the impossible though neither of us wanted to accept that. The following months involved emotional circular discussions starting with my need to stop and finishing with the obvious fact I couldn't because of our financial position. However, my health was deteriorating and I was literally coming to a standstill.

Eventually I stopped. In August 2009 I hit a crisis point, I could no longer carry on and I started a long term sabbatical from the Bar. Over the following months whilst I held down a tutoring post at the University (which I loved) the rest of the time I felt like all my energy had been sapped from me and I experienced the most dreadful pain. It was like living with the worst possible type of 'flu. In March 2010 I was diagnosed with Chronic Fatigue. It was quite possibly the best thing to have happened, although I could barely walk 100m and taking the children to school had become exhausting. Finally, I had the chance to stop, to become the person I wanted to be.

I can only describe this part of my journey to be like peeling layers of an onion off one by one – there were lots of them, they were difficult to peel and many of them may make you cry! I realised that I had become completely depersonalised over the previous ten years –I would have to start to live – to feed my soul – to change my life. I decided to wind up my legal practice completely – a decision that would define my recovery – I could finally become better as there was now no expectation of a return to the person that I had been before.

My heart was telling me to pursue something completely different, reflexology, which sounded complete madness! I'm sure that those around me thought I had had some kind of breakdown, I hadn't at all, but I had to agree it was the antipathy of Law! I started with a holistic massage course at a local college and even shocked myself when I found it really made my heart start to sing! This was closely followed by me undertaking a Reflexology Diploma at Jubilee College and in July 2012 Eden House Holistic opened for business.

Whilst physically my day to day was changing, so was I on the inside. I exposed myself to everything and anything – neurolinguistic programming, hypnotherapy, mindfulness, meditation, yoga, pilates, reiki and many more, both with practitioners and many, many books. The biggest change was that I no longer allowed others to influence my decisions – I realised that I had attracted many strong characters in my life who were quick to judge and quick to criticise my judgement. I decided, if I was happy with my decision, then I needed no further approval. Over the last four years, my judgement has proved to be sound and that now is good enough for me!

Today I can honestly say, that for the first time in many, many years I am happy and content. When people who haven't seen me for some time meet me, the first thing they comment on is that I look so well and happy! I don't know what the future holds but I no longer worry about it; I see challenges as opportunities a chance to grow even more! I now have a successful therapy business, I run our local Professional Reflexology Group which is thriving and in the New Year I am launching an online Holistic Therapy resource which is extremely exciting! But above all we have a happy family! What's not to look forward to!!

One thing that my life has taught me, is that life is a journey, there are lessons to be learnt, but it is there to be enjoyed, no decision is truly final and where there is an end there is undoubtedly always a beginning.

Contents

Foreword

Lesson One – Remember the me that you want to be!

Lesson Two – Observe!

Lesson Three – Smile!

Lesson Four – just a little thanks….

Lesson 5 – The perfect way to start the day!

Lesson Six – Breaking the same old same old…

Lesson Seven – Compassion

Lesson Eight – Do a Random Act of Kindness

Lesson Nine – Do something that makes you laugh!

Lesson Ten – Be realistic not perfect!

Lesson Eleven – Learn to breathe.

Lesson Twelve – Finishing your day

Lesson Thirteen – Positively reflecting

Lesson Fourteen – Find your voice!

Lesson Fifteen – Choose your battles!

Lesson Sixteen – Big white fluffy things!

Lesson Seventeen – Clear the decks!

Lesson Eighteen – You will always be right!

Lesson Nineteen – D.I.S.C.O

Lesson Twenty – Meditation for the Sole.

Lesson Twenty One – Focus on YOU!

Lesson Twenty Two – Identify your flash points.

Lesson Twenty Three – Invest in YOU!

Lesson Twenty Four – Don't put off till tomorrow what you can do today!!!

Lesson Twenty Five – Make life interesting!

Lesson Twenty Six – Focus on NOW!

Lesson Twenty Seven – It's a natural thing!

Lesson Twenty Eight – Change your environment!

Lesson Twenty Nine – A gift from you..

Lesson Thirty – Wonder at the greatness of it all..

Foreword

Five years ago I wasn't happy. In fact on a bad day you could catch me saying perhaps I just wasn't meant to be happy, or I just wasn't a happy person – it was just the way I was made. I was in a job I no longer enjoyed, I had a family I didn't see and I felt that I was really not very good at anything. Then things got worse, I contracted pneumonia and developed ME. I slowly ground to a halt.

This was the best thing that has ever happened to me . It actually allowed me the time to really think about who I wanted to be and also, how to go about achieving it!!

Now I live a very happy life – in fact I am one of the happiest people I know! Don't get me wrong I haven't won the lottery or married a business tycoon living the life of luxury; but I am happy.

Through this book, I wanted to share some of the tools that I use to achieve such a positive outlook. It isn't a weighty thesis, and nor will it give you all of the answers. It's more of an introduction to how you can regain control of your own mindset and develop your 'Feel Good' factor.

I love books that I can just dip into, so it was always going to be the case that I would write a 'dip in' book! With the exception of the first few 'lessons' you can do just that! So you can keep it by your bed, your sofa or even your loo and dip into it when you can – or you can opt to take one 'lesson' a day.

You may find that some of the chapters suit you better, or some are more difficult than others, but I hope that this starts you on a journey towards making your life a happier place.

Andrea

Lesson One – Remember the me that you want to be!

'Remember me with smiles and laughter, for that is how I will remember you all. If you can only remember me with tears, then don't remember me at all.'

Laura Ingalls Wilder

'Today is the first day of the rest of your life!' I can't remember who said that, but it was someone famous! Well today, is the first day of the rest of your 'happy' life, but new habits take time and old ones are hard to break. So although today's lesson is easy it is very important as it will remind you that you are on a new journey.

First, you need to make the decision that from today you are going to make the effort to be happy and positive. Everyone deserves to be happy, even you and yes you are allowed to be happy! Have you ever thought I'll be happy when....I get a new job, the kids start school/leave home, we move house, I have no debts or something similar? Well, guess what, my view is that none of those things will make you happy, because when they happen, there will be something else that your happiness will depend on, because happiness comes from inside you. Therefore you have to decide to be happy and until you make that decision, nothing external to you will make you happy.

Unfortunately, we do live in a society which points out the negative in practically all things and often it is very difficult to remain positive when faced with an abundance of negativity – it can be quite contagious. So secondly, find something that helps you remember to 'remember the me that you want to be'. Something that will remind you to be positive when faced with the negativity of life, or when you are getting stressed or feeling overwhelmed.

This could be a picture that you place in a prominent position, it could be little smiley face stickers that you put all over the place, such as a mirror, your purse, or the front door. It could be a piece of jewellery that you wear all the time (I have a ring that I wear that I bought in memory of a dear friend who was a lovely happy person – it reminds me to be more like her!) It doesn't matter what it is, there is no right or wrong, what does matter is that today you made the decision that you wanted to be happy and positive and your chosen reminder will remind you of that - so that when you find yourself slipping back, it will help you to stop being so negative!

Lesson Two – Observe!

'I think it's important to get your surroundings as well as yourself into a positive state - meaning surround yourself with positive people, not the kind who are negative and jealous of everything you do.'

Heidi Klum

This can be a tricky one. Try to imagine that everyone around you has to pass a positivity test and that you are the examiner. Please don't tell them that this is what you are doing, as they may be offended if they fail, just silently observe the people around you.

What is their general topic of conversation – are they moaning? Do they look at the world in a glass half empty type way? Do they have nothing good to say about people who are in a better position than them? Do they always look for problems and not solutions – even if you suggest a solution will they find a problem with the solution?

A friend of mine explained to me once that negative people are like drains (positive people are like radiators!).

Negative people are like drains because they suck any positivity out of you and leave you feeling worse than you did when you started talking to them. They can always find the negative in every situation or person – they really do love a good moan! This is a good way to identify a 'drain' – how do you feel after being with them? Do you feel drained? Down in the dumps? Despondent? Or do you feel on top of the world? Inspired? Positive?

Positive people are the exact opposite, they radiate positivity and make you feel so much better when you speak to them. They always look for the best, even when it is hard to find. You feel like there are always options and that you can resolve whatever issues you are facing.

If you imagine a spiral, when you are surrounded by negative people you will spiral downwards towards negativity, if you surround yourself with positive people you spiral upwards towards positivity.

Generally speaking positive people attract positive people, and negative people attract negative people.

So if you want to be more positive, guess who you have to surround yourself with??

The other trick is if you want to surround yourself with positive people – be more positive!! However, if you find yourself unexpectedly in conversation with a negative person, just don't get sucked into their 'neg-fest', there is no point trying to convince them that they are wrong or adopt a more positive view – they will only try to convince you that you are wrong! My tactic, is just to politely excuse myself and remember that it is important that I make my own mind up about a situation or a person as negative people often have their own agenda and by subscribing to it the view is unlikely to be balanced – or positive!!

Now, I'm not suggesting that you now delete everyone off your friends list, but it is useful to be aware of how positive those around you are so that you can be aware of how it can affect your own outlook – it may be that on days when you are not feeling so positive you will try to be amongst more positive people than negative!

Lesson Three – Smile!

'Let us always meet each other with smile, for the smile is the beginning of love.'

Mother Teresa

You may think that this is easy peasy, but actually it may be more difficult than you think.

First of all take some time to think about how often you actually smile. I sat on a bus once and looked at the people around me, I then walked through town and I was struck by how little people actually smile. I read once somewhere that it takes more muscles to frown than it does to smile so it actually causes more wrinkles so it's really much better on lots of levels to smile!!!

Here are some more things for you to think about.

For today, decide to smile more, use something to remind you to smile (smiley face stickers are good for this!)

Notice – how do you feel when you smile? The chances are that you will feel better. This is definitely the case if you do it privately in front of a mirror because you will feel silly and smile more as you laugh at yourself!

Next, notice the people around you - what happens when you smile at a Checkout Assistant when you say thank you? Or when you are at work, and you smile at a colleague, when you say hello? Or just when you are walking down the street and smile as you say hello to a passer-by?

The chances are that they will smile too!!! So not only are you making yourself feel better – but you are making those around you feel better too!

Smiles are very powerful tools, think about what we said before about drains and radiators and the upward spiral of positivity – think about the effect that smiling could have just on your work place – or if you are in contact with the general public.

Try it and see what happens!

Lesson Four – just a little thanks….

'Thank you is the best prayer that anyone could say. I say that one a lot. Thank you expresses extreme gratitude, humility, understanding.'

Alice Walker

Life is so busy, we just rush from one thing to the next, grabbing items from the supermarket, giving directions at work, telling uncontrollable children where they should be or what they should be doing – the list is endless.

Today, just take a moment to think of how many times you interact with people – how many times did you say thank you? If you did say thank you, then how did you say it?

We underestimate this totally in our society, we do take – a lot, and we moan a lot about what we have taken. We can always find fault with what people have done or not done in our opinion, what they should be doing or how they should be doing it.

Today, just be thankful for what they have done. Recognise what the people around you are contributing, however little that may be. Not only will you feel better for it, but also those around you are more likely to do more (remember those radiators and drains!). Just think, how do you feel when you are unappreciated or criticised – how do you react when you are praised or thanked? So the next time that you are being served at a shop or restaurant, thank the assistants properly – take some time to do it. Not just a quick 'thanks for that' but 'thank you for the service today it was great' or 'thank you – hope you have a good day too'. It takes minutes but potentially can make big differences – if nothing else to the way you feel!! Notice what that person does, I would guess that 99.9% of the time they SMILE!!

On a personal note, this has made a big difference to my family, in the dark ages, I was always focussing on what hadn't been done by my patient other half (some may say that I slip and still do it occasionally now). This is often because the one thing that hasn't been done is the one thing that you need to be done, but recognising and being thankful for all the other stuff really makes you think about how you react to that one thing that's annoyed you. It's called getting it all into perspective and being thankful really helps with this!

Lesson 5 – The perfect way to start the day!

'Everyone has highs and lows that they have to learn from, but every morning I start off with a good head on my shoulders, saying to myself, It's going to be a good day!'

Lindsay Lohan

How do you normally start the day – before you even open your eyes that is?

Do you have a feeling of impending dread, run through all those horrible things you have been putting off all week, all month, or even all year?

Do you open your eyes wishing that you could just pull the duvet over your head and forget that the world existed? Today's lesson won't change your life, but it might make you feel a bit better about what you have to deal with today.

Before you open your eyes, remember five things that you are really grateful for. Do this every day, the first thing that you need to ask yourself is 'what can I be grateful for today?'

There is no right answer, it could be anything, it could be a holiday that you've booked, it could be that your child has woken to see another day or that you have. It could be the air that you breathe, the roof over your head, or it may even be the smell of the latte that your kind other half is making for you! It can be five really small things, they don't have to be huge, sometimes remembering the small things is really important.

I started doing this and initially I thought I had little to be grateful for, ok I had a house, a husband, lovely kids but anything else? So I started to write them down (obviously I was awake at this point) and I was staggered at how much I had to be grateful for, I started to look at the real detail of my life, not just the big things or the material things and it really changed my focus – if you think about it five new things over a month, two months, a year, soon adds up.

So if you do this every day, before too long, as you open your eyes, you may even start to smile!

Lesson Six – Breaking the same old same old...

'Everyone thinks of changing the world, but no one thinks of changing himself.'

Leo Tolstoy

Do you ever feel like every day is just a re-run of the day before? That you are on a perpetual treadmill never getting anywhere?

Well today do something different!

You may still have to go to work, take the kids to school/nursery, go to the supermarket, do ten loads of washing etc etc. But at lunchtime or in a break or just for five minutes *do something different!* It might be that you read a bit of a book in a local park, have a coffee in a different café, walk around an art gallery for fifteen minutes or simply just walk a different way to work. You could buy yourself some flowers, make a card, plant a geranium, go for a run, take the dog for a walk somewhere different. It can be absolutely anything.

It could be something that you enjoyed when you were younger, maybe a hobby or pastime, or something you've been meaning to do for a while.

Change your routine – just a tiny bit and start to **live** your day!

I realised that I was so bogged down with life, I didn't know what my favourite music was, I hadn't read a book in ages, I didn't have a favourite restaurant or park, I hadn't even really explored where I lived even though I'd lived there for nearly 6 years. I worked, I slept, I looked after the children and although the latter gave me enormous joy, I wasn't really living! So I took one step at a time at living! I started to take up hobbies, listen to music, I took courses in writing poetry (yes that one is true albeit slightly unbelievable!) But slowly, all these things made me feel like I was actually alive, it was a chance to get off the hamster wheel of life even though it was only for a short time.

So one small change can make a big difference to your day! Once you've done it once, carry on doing it, decide what you are going to do tomorrow, the next day – those precious few moments when you do something different will become one of the highlights of your day! And you may even get to know yourself a little better!

Lesson Seven – Compassion

'If you want others to be happy, practice compassion. If you want to be happy, practice compassion.'

Dalai Lama

Life can be really hard and sometimes people are like houses – the outside can look really good, but you open the front door and what lies behind tells a very different story.

None of us really know what it is like to be someone else, yet many of us think it is absolutely fine to judge our fellow man.

What has this got to do with my happiness, you might ask?

In my own personal experience when I started becoming more compassionate to other people, I began to be more compassionate towards myself and that made a huge difference to my own personal happiness! You might think that this is a really selfish attitude and you may be right, but it is a pretty good place to start. What I found was that because I judged others I naturally assumed others would be assessing me; this led me to judge myself in order to counteract this. When I stopped rating others and became more compassionate and understanding towards them I naturally cared less about what others thought about me (because generally those types of people would be negative people anyway) and I began to become more compassionate about myself as I was being towards other people.

So how can you go about this?

Well the next time you make a judgement about someone else – it might be about their behaviour, or what they have said, or the clothes they wear or the standard of their work. Just take a moment to think about why they might have behaved or chosen to do something, whatever it is, in that way. Put yourself in their shoes for that moment and consider what it might be like for them. What could have caused them to behave in this way? How would you feel if you were in that position? How would you like to be treated? If you don't know or can't imagine, do you really have the right to make that assessment? If you don't, then quite simply, don't do it.

Instead of making that negative judgement, think something positive about them instead. For example, if someone contributes to a conversation and they say something inappropriate – instead of criticising them and deciding they obviously only have three brain cells, explain to yourself that they must be really nervous or have misunderstood the conversation. Ask yourself if there is anything you can do to put them at their ease, or can you help them in any way? If someone's children are playing up or having a tantrum, instead of criticising their parenting skills consider that they must be really stressed or having a bad day – or well that's what kids do, isn't it! Or, think what you would like someone to do, to help you – if you are in a supermarket and the parent is struggling with a trolley – you might think to ask if you can help! Do something positive instead of simply staring and judging!

The more you make yourself stop and think about this, the more you may realise how many times a day you judge – or pass comment on another person.

If you are in a work situation it can be even more apparent, remember the earlier chapter about drains and the effect negative people have on those around them – judging is a negative behaviour. How do you view your work colleagues? Do you talk about them to other colleagues? Do you criticise them? Find fault with what they do?

If possible instead of berating someone, either to their face or otherwise, for making a mistake, act sensitively asking why this might have happened and try to move the situation forward positively. Act with compassion – don't jump to the conclusion that it was because they were simply rubbish! But of course, I could probably write a whole book on how to deal effectively with employee relationships!

So you get the picture, try not to pass judgement at all, but if you have to, try to act sympathetically and with empathy. Remember when you see a person you only get to see what they let you see and that is usually not the full story.

Lesson Eight – Do a random act of kindness

'Carry out a random act of kindness, with no expectation of reward, safe in the knowledge that one day someone might do the same for you.'

Princess Diana

How many times have you been the passer-by in a situation? Someone might have dropped their shopping, or some documents, a child might have fallen over, they might have been taken ill whilst you've been out and about, or a neighbour or someone where you live might have been taken ill or had an accident.

How did you react? What did you do? Did you just pretend not to see or know about it and do nothing?

Well today, see if you can think of some random act of kindness that you can do.

It might be a neighbour who you know doesn't get very many visitors – go and take them some flowers or invite them over for a cup of tea.

Buy a good friend a gift, just to say thank you for being there, run your partner a bath or pour them their favourite drink. Or you can look after a friend's baby so they can have some respite? Take a meal to someone who has just come out of hospital?

If you see a situation that requires help (not a dangerous one obviously or one where clearly your help would not be welcome!) go and offer your services!

There is no right or wrong, but it does require us to think outside of our own needs and think about other people and the challenges that they face. Ask yourself, can I help them or can I do anything that could make them feel better even if it is just momentarily or just so they know someone is thinking about them?

One option is to do something for a charity or volunteer for a community project I'm sure that there are lots of organisations locally that would be so grateful for some of your time – often volunteers are very few and far between.

The act of giving is a very powerful tool. I can't point you to any indisputable evidence that this is the case – but try it for yourself and really take note of how it makes you feel to give and watch the response of your action from the people that it affects. As I said, it requires you to think outside of yourself, which when we are in a negative place is not easy to do, but I think is almost essential if we are to move to a more positive place.

Quite often, the gift of giving involves the one thing that is free – time and we should never be caught saying that we can't give any of our time to other human beings. Often, just a short amount of time can make a huge difference.

Lesson Nine – Do something that makes you laugh!

'Laugh, and the world laughs with you;
Weep, and you weep alone.'

Ella Wheeler Wilcox

Today's lesson is really easy, all you need to do is find something that really makes you laugh, giggle, guffaw, chuckle, split your sides or whatever else you want to call it!

I have found that generally speaking we all take life a little too seriously! We are all on this earth for such a short space of time and it goes so quickly – what a shame to spend it being miserable and deathly serious!

Watch a comedy, go out with a good friend, find something funny on YouTube, play a silly game with your kids. Have a tickling fest, a pillow fight, play balloon volleyball. But take time out to laugh!

Just think how good you would feel if every day you went to bed knowing that something that day had really made you laugh!

If you can't actually do something, then look out for something during the day that makes you laugh – nature is a great source of inspiration – pigeons trying to pick up heavy sandwiches, a dog being bullied by a cat. I know it sounds utterly ridiculous, but if it helps, just laugh at how rubbish my suggestions are!

When we laugh we produce endorphins – the happy hormone – so it really does make you feel a whole lot better!!!

And if all else fails FAKE it!

Seriously, just laugh, really belly laugh!

Lesson Ten – Be realistic, not perfect!

'We have to be realistic. If we don't win, life will continue.'
Hayden Fry

Think about what causes your stress – make sure that it isn't your expectations!

Consider this – do you expect your car to start every morning? How old is it? Do you look after it? Or do you just expect every morning year after year for it to faithfully start??

Do you expect your children to wake up happy and refreshed eager to please you by getting dressed in record time and eat their breakfast without a fuss – remembering all the things they need for school?

Do you expect your alarm to go off at the right time every morning without fail?

How do you react when your car doesn't start? Your kids act like children? You forget to plug your phone in so your alarm doesn't go off because your battery is flat?

STRESSED! It's the worst day EVER!!!

Sometimes we create our own stress – our own unhappiness – because we expect life to run smoothly all of the time, and guess what? It doesn't!!

So today, try and alter your expectations and see what happens!! Cars sometimes don't start, trains/buses are often late, there are traffic jams, accidents, children forget a whole array of stuff that they then urgently need two minutes before they leave for school.

Learn to repeat the mantra 'Ok these things happen,' instead of questioning 'Why does this always happen to me?' or similar.

A couple of tricks that I use are, if I'm stuck in traffic – let's face it there's nothing you can do – so I view it as a gift of time. I turn the radio or CD up and I enjoy that space in my day. If the car doesn't start – adopt the same view. What can you do? You ring the recovery people, let it be known you'll be late – then make yourself a sneaky coffee! Enjoy the time!!

Kids forget stuff all the time, they are late, disorganised, often crotchety and disobedient (or is that just mine). Accept that as a fact and reflect on how you can reduce the stress – list what you need each day, try to leave slightly earlier to give yourself some breathing space and just keep saying 'we're fine!'!!

Take a deep breath and don't let it spoil your day you'll never have this day again!

Lesson Eleven – Learn to breathe.

'Breathe. Let go. And remind yourself that this very moment is the only one you know you have for sure.'
Oprah Winfrey

Ok, so you've been breathing for a long time now and you think that you're really good at it? But are you really? A variety of different people have used the concept of breathing deeply and you may have come across it during a pilates or yoga class. Well guess what you can use it at other times as well – in fact I use it most of the time!!!

Breathing properly is a great tool for stress relief as it can have the effect of lowering that feeling of adrenaline rushing around in our bodies. You can also use it as part of a meditation or even when things are just getting too much as something to focus on to calm you down. The great thing is that you can do it anywhere – you don't need a special mat or space, which means you can do it on a bus, in a queue, sat at your computer – you just need to take a couple of minutes to concentrate on it.

This is how you do it.

First of all place one hand on the area just under your rib cage (where your diaphragm is) and one on your chest area.

Breathe in slowly. Note which hand rises, is it your lower hand or the one on your chest?

Now breathe out slowly, and when you are ready, breathe in again and try to focus on keeping the hand on your chest as still as you can and instead concentrate on making the lower hand rise as your abdomen starts to swell.

This may take quite a bit of practice and that's ok, it can take time to master this art, but you can practice it anywhere – just place your hand on the area below your ribs and concentrate on lifting it away from your body as you breathe in.

Happy breathing and enjoy!

Lesson Twelve – Finishing your day

'Being the richest man in the cemetery doesn't matter to me. Going to bed at night saying we've done something wonderful, that's what matters to me.'

Steve Jobs

I always think it is so important to finish the day on a good note but so many people underestimate how vital it is to your overall feeling of well being. Just think for a minute how many times have you had a bad day and gone to bed still chewing things over then woken up the next day feeling exactly the same – even though this is a new day! Wouldn't it be great to start each new day on a new fresh positive note, instead of dragging the previous day into it?

One way to help with this is to finish your day positively. So before you go to sleep think about the most positive thing or the best thing that happened that day, or perhaps the one thing that you were glad about happening, or perhaps it was something that you thought would go wrong that didn't or something completely unexpected that happened like meeting an old friend or colleague.

It doesn't matter how big or small it is – it could just have been that your son or daughter gave you the biggest hug or that your dog greeted you like you were the best owner in the world. Or it could have been that you got a pay rise or you were offered a new job opportunity!

The main thing is, is that the last thing that you think about is positive! So if your mind wanders to worries or problems – pull your mind back to the good stuff – end your day on a positive note so that you are giving tomorrow the best chance of being a new day!

Lesson Thirteen – Positively Reflecting

'We should regret our mistakes and learn from them, but never carry them forward into the future with us'.

Lucy Maud Montgomery

Believe it or not we all make mistakes, even me! Things may not go as planned or we may simply have got something wrong. It happens because none of us are perfect but we often don't tell ourselves that. We expect ourselves to be perfect and when we make a mistake we beat ourselves up over it. The trick is not to do this but to learn from it.

Of course when we are very young we're told, 'We all make mistakes, you just have to learn from them' but do we? And how do we avoid falling into a negative spiral where we tell ourselves that we are no good at what we do, we shouldn't even try, it always goes wrong etc. etc.

Reflecting positively is a very good start to stopping this spiral!

First of all, ask yourself what you were expecting to happen and then secondly, what did happen.

If what happened wasn't what you expected, ask yourself why you think that is? Why did it happen in that way?

The next part is the most important. Often after we have thought about what has happened and what we thought would happen our next step is to move in a negative direction – we might tell ourselves how rubbish we are or how we are never going to do it again, it always happens like that, we are completely useless.

Stop! At this point, we positively reflect. Instead of beating yourself up, ask yourself what you would do differently *next* time. Because there is going to be a next time! This is your learning phase, where you put steps in place to help you grow as a person and move forward.

We all make mistakes, it is a fact of life, but it is how you deal with them that is key – make it a positive experience, sometimes we make mistakes so that we learn lessons, important lessons that direct our lives in a positive way, so they are not all bad! Often I reflect on the mistakes I've made and I realise that they were some of the best things that happened as I learnt a lot and also other things happened as a result!

Lesson Fourteen – Find your voice!

'What a liberation to realize that the 'voice in my head' is not who I am. 'Who am I, then?' The one who sees that.'

Eckhart Tolle

We all have a voice in our head! No I haven't lost the plot you know what I'm talking about, it's the voice that often chunters away. What does your voice say to you? Perhaps it is encouraging and supporting – or does it tell you that this will never work and what you're doing is a lot of rubbish?

Sometimes what we tell ourselves has a real effect on how we feel – and guess what it's our head, our voice so, unless you have a medical condition, you're in control!

I was introduced to the following technique when I did a short spell in sales and spoke to other colleagues about how they controlled that nagging doubt that we all get from time to time. (Actually mine was quite an authoritative doubting voice which I had lived with for a good few years!)

First of all, have a good listen to that voice – what does it sound like, is it authoritative or unsure – parent or childlike?

What do you think the voice would look like? Try to have a picture in your mind of that person (mine is like an old bitter granny with little glasses that she peers through!).

Now give it a name (I call her Mildred).

So now you should be able to visualise the voice, think of it as a separate person to you – and now it's time to challenge it.

Often I find that Mildred can make sweeping statements – 'It never goes right for me, don't bother, it won't turn out right, it won't be successful.' You need to challenge this – 'is that right?' 'is it really never?', never is a very absolute term, if you think hard, you will find a time when something did go right for you.

The voice may try to look into the future? As above, it might say that 'it won't turn out right, things won't be successful' or 'It's going to be terrible!' – challenge it! 'Can you really look into the future?' Do you really know for certain that it won't go right, that things will be terrible – it may well go brilliantly well, this could be a fantastic success if you gave it a chance especially if you have been practising positive reflection!

Or your voice may try and read minds! 'That person thinks I'm rubbish/doesn't like me/thinks they are better than me etc.' – you just need to challenge it. 'How do you know what that person is thinking? Can you read their mind? For all you know they are worried about their own situation, and not the slightest bit concerned about you. They could be thinking how great you are and wondering how on earth they can improve themselves!

Each time it happens challenge your own Mildred, she will soon get bored and you will find that voice will slowly be replaced by a more coaching, positive voice. How do I know? After a long time of doing this, I was faced with quite a challenging situation, a situation which at one time I would have made excuses and tried to get out of. However, I found myself coaching myself, telling myself it would be fine, I was prepared and I was going to be great – and you know it was and I really enjoyed it!

Lesson Fifteen – Choose your battles!

'Pick battles big enough to matter, small enough to win.'

Jonathan Kozol

Do you sometimes feel that you have to battle for everything? Do you find yourself asking 'Why don't people just do what they are supposed to do?' Or do you find yourself frequently making complaints?

How does it make you feel when you complain? Or when you have to argue a point? Or convince someone that they have made a mistake? On the whole, when we are in this position our stress responses kick in – not our happy hormones!

Guess what? You have a choice – you can choose which battle to fight!

Often in life we get so caught up with being right and arguing a point of principle that we forget to sit back and ask whether it is in actual fact worth it!! Most of the time it isn't! So what if your coffee wasn't as hot as it should be or the bus was late, or our hotel room wasn't spotless or you just think you ought to have been treated better? Is it really worth getting all steamed up over??

Sometimes before we dive in with a raging argument it is worth spending some time considering what we will achieve (or what we would like to achieve) and balance this against any stress or negativity that the argument will cause. Ask yourself is arguing this principle really worth the emotional (and maybe if it is really stressful, physical) cost.

In fact, I have learnt quite recently that often it is quite empowering to simply walk away!

Lesson Sixteen – Big white fluffy things!

'Rest is not idleness, and to lie sometimes on the grass under trees on a summer's day, listening to the murmur of the water, or watching the clouds float across the sky, is by no means a waste of time.'

John Lubbock

When you were little did you look at the sky and cloud watch? Just look at them and try and spot things like elephants, tea cups, Great Uncle Fred?

Today's lesson is a bit like that. Take some time to look at the sky – especially if it is a lovely blue sunny sky – think about the magnitude of it, the colour – how amazing it is that when we look up we see a cover that can be blues, pinks, whites, yet from the moon we see right through it to the earth. When you start, you really will begin to be in awe of its total magnitude and beauty.

Now for fun (because life should be fun not an endurance test!) do some good old fashioned cloud watching! Watch the clouds, the shapes they form, their texture, their colour, their size. What do they remind you of? Look at them move, are they floating fast or slow, are they low in the sky or high?

Just really take some time out to wonder at them!

Lesson Seventeen – Clear the decks!

'Cleaning is my favorite way to relax. I clear things out and get rid of the stuff I don't need. When the food pantry and the refrigerator are organized, I feel less stressed.'

Jennifer Morrison

I absolutely love having a good clear out, it makes me feel as though I am back in the driving seat and not drowning in lots of stuff! So today's lesson is all about having a good old fashioned clear out – it could be a drawer, a cupboard, a box with stuff in or a whole room if you are up to it! Or whatever is bugging you (I sometimes find that my email inbox can be enormously irritating and I get great satisfaction from deleting all the rubbish!) – I call them pockets of disorganisation – one is usually found on the corner of my kitchen worktop!

I find that for a reasonable sized clear out having three bags on the go helps – one for rubbish, one for charity and one for recycling (remember to leave time to actually get rid of it as you may find it all creeps back in again (especially if you have little helpers!).

If you really don't like doing this sort of thing there are a few motivational tricks you can use.

The first one is to give yourself a time limit – however long you want to spend on the task not how long you think it will take (as we usually think it will take forever!) – fifteen minutes, half an hour – if you have a timer, put it on and see if you can do it in this time. At least you know then there's going to be an end to it and you can do other things afterwards.

The second tip, is to think of a really good reward – nice coffee, piece of cake, or whatever floats your boat! But something to give you a big well done when you've finished!

And lastly, put on some really motivational music!! Something that really lifts your spirits, makes you want to dance around or even sing – lighten the mood and enjoy yourself! Honestly it really does help!

Lesson Eighteen – You will always be right!

'Whether you believe you can do a thing or not, you are right.'

Henry Ford

This is such a common trait, that even I have to still stop myself from doing this! Do you ever find yourself either saying to a friend or to yourself statements like – 'I'm going to be so tired tomorrow after this' or 'I'm going to be so nervous / stressed / sick / bad tempered…..'

We do it so naturally, we second guess how we (or actually sometimes those around us) are going to behave (it's even more likely to happen with children when we second guess that they are going to behave badly). Guess what, when we make these statements we will be right, we will feel / behave like that or those around us will behave like it!

I believe the reason for this is because, without realising it, we then look, for evidence to support that belief and we fail to recognise the evidence that supports the opposite perspective.

So take for example the child who has been to a party and you know that they have had all sorts of yummy sugary things and exhausted themselves on a bouncy castle – you say to yourself 'Grrr, they are going to be a nightmare!' Guess what they will be because you will spot any bad behaviour to support that and ignore the cuddle they gave a sibling, how they helped you clear the table, or put their shoes away or even drew you a picture. In fact you will ignore any good behaviour *but* you will remember all the bad stuff – the fact they didn't want to leave the party, they spilt a drink when they got home, they didn't want to go to bed, they screamed for ten minutes and threw their toys around, etc. etc. etc. – because you will always be right!!!

Or have you ever had to give a presentation to a bunch of really important people? You sit in the toilet beforehand running through all the stuff that is bound to go wrong. You tell yourself, I won't be able to read my notes, the projector won't work, I'll fiddle with my hands, I'll mumble and stutter like I did the last time (Mildred has a real field day at times like these). Are you really going to give the most fantastic presentation you have ever done with all this floating around your head? NO! You will go in, your body full of adrenaline, you won't be thinking clearly, you'll panic you can't find your notes, let alone read them. This will be the start of the evidence gathering phase – you tell yourself 'I told you this would happen', you try the laptop but it won't switch on 'See' you tell yourself 'it won't work!' (mainly because it is not plugged in) and so it goes on. You will be right!

So if you are always right, you can just change the prophecy – there is no rule to say that a self-fulfilling prophecy has to be a negative one! So just change the messages that you tell yourself.

Instead of telling yourself all the things that will go wrong, you tell yourself all the things that will go right!!! 'I'll be fine' 'I'm prepared' 'It will all work out ok'. Guess what – you go into the presentation calm, you spot that your notes are in a different folder, the laptop is unplugged, etc etc. Or you tell yourself your child will be fine, they always are, you will start to notice the good stuff so that when things go awry they aren't as major. . .

Make positive statements about yourself and you, and other people will be surprised at the results!

Lesson Nineteen – D.I.S.C.O

*'She is D, delirious
She is I, incredible
She is S, superficial
She is C, complicated
She is O, oh, oh, oh'*

Ottawan

You are probably thinking, she's halfway through the book and she's running out of ideas! I haven't though, honestly! But music plays a big part in my life and I find it really affects how you can feel.

So, if you have a task ahead of you that is dragging you down or you are putting it off or if you are feeling stressed about something playing music can really help!

Obviously you need to choose the music to fit the situation – no rock and roll if you are trying to write a tricky report (but if it works for you, who am I to dictate?)

You will often find me in the kitchen, either cooking or cleaning (or decorating) with music that I can dance to blaring out. This is to the embarrassment of my kids when I ask them to dance with me. As they get older they have become less obliging, but when they do, we find ourselves rolling around giggling. However, I find that afterwards, whatever it was that I had to do is done quicker and with far more grace! It really lifts the mood, everyone is happier and we've had some fun (and isn't that what life is all about?).

Equally, if I have a difficult piece of work to do, then putting some chilling music can help too, it quietens my stress responses so that I can concentrate on what I have to do.

So now's the time to go through your music collection and dig out those tunes – nothing like having a bit of a bop to something you loved when you were younger!!

Lesson Twenty – Meditation for the Sole.

'To me a lush carpet of pine needles or spongy grass is more welcome than the most luxurious Persian rug.'

Helen Keller

As you might have read, I am a Reflexologist and so I love feet! There is just something about them, especially, how they are usually the one thing that connects you to the earth.

This is really an exercise in being quiet and also connecting. It is very simple, but once you start it can get a little addictive!!

First of all, take off your shoes and socks. Find somewhere to stand – preferably outside if it is warm enough and even better if it is on grass (just make sure that the area is clear from anything sharp or nasty!)

Take a moment to wriggle your toes and feel the grass under your feet, make sure that you are standing comfortably.

Close your eyes, and practice the breathing that we discussed earlier.

Now while you are breathing, really concentrate on your feet and what you can feel. What does it feel like when you stretch out your toes? Now try wriggling them? Maybe shift the weight from one to the other?

Now open your eyes and just walk around slowly, but keep thinking about your feet, what are they doing?

Concentrate and think about how your weight is shifting, what touches the ground first your heels or your toes? What does the grass feel like, where is the grass touching? Is it cold or warm? All the time, think about how your feet are feeling and how they are connecting to the earth.

Definitely meditation for the *sole!*

Lesson Twenty One – Focus on YOU!

'The worst thing I can be is the same as everybody else. I hate that.'

Arnold Schwarzenegger

Ok, so you've been to a friend's house for a coffee, or met a colleague for lunch, and you've spent an hour listening to how they have just got a new car, they've been on a fabulous holiday, their partner has a fantastic new job, they've paid their mortgage off and you come away feeling like they have a great life and quite frankly yours is tough.

Stop there!

Why are you worried about what someone else has? First of all, the vast majority of the time you never get the full story. I remember a long time ago thinking that someone I knew had it all, they were beautiful, had a lovely home, great job, loads of money, wealthy husband etc. etc., only to find out later that actually they were deeply unhappy, her husband had loads of affairs, they didn't own their house and were actually in a lot of debt. Life isn't always what it seems. I always think people are like houses – you can go up to the front of a house and it might look fantastic, but you have no idea what is behind the front door – you can imagine it is just as beautiful, but it may not be.

So with this in mind, is it really useful to hanker over other people's lives? Does it really help you in any way? The answer clearly is no (and if you think yes, please think really hard about it!)

What is important is what you do, and how you are. We all make choices in our lives, you may not have a flash car, go on three holidays a year to sunnier climes, but you will have other things that those people don't have – things that are important to you because you have given them priority over other, often more material stuff.

So today, just worry about you, and be true to yourself. If you make a decision that you are happy about, then don't worry about what other people do, because it doesn't change the choices that you want to make – that's their life, not yours! I always like to think that we are all on a journey, and decisions that other people make relate to the journey that they are on, you may not be on the same journey so it really doesn't matter what they do.

If there are things that you want to change, then put steps in place to change them – but don't base these on other people's choices, take these steps because you want to, not because you are comparing your life with them.

Lesson Twenty Two – Identify your flash points.

'If it all just happens like this for the rest of my life, it's going to be one endless Groundhog Day. I determined that I was not prepared to submit to this regime, so I thought I had to do something about it.'

Bruce Dickinson

Do some days just seem like ground hog day? You get up (often a bit late because you are tired because you didn't get to bed), you make coffee but when you open the cupboard several other boxes fall out), you can't find your favourite cup because it is upstairs where you left it from yesterday. You trundle back upstairs to face the waking family, then the chaos really starts! You can't find uniforms, something hasn't been washed, it's French day and no one told you, you start to get ready, but then someone else has a meltdown, there's no bread for the packed lunches, you can't find anything to wear to work, your wardrobe is jammed packed, the ironing's not done, and you can't get a drawer open! You all end up being late, you've had no breakfast and you feel like you've done a day's work and the kids aren't at school yet!

Ok, so this might just be my house! But think about it, what can you do to minimise this sort of scenario?

We are all human, we run out of stuff, we forget to go shopping, we have late nights, our kids don't tell us stuff, we are not perfect! But we can try to lower the stress levels by being a little more organised and identifying those things that make us more stressed than we need to be!

If something happens regularly that causes you stress, I term it a flash point and if it can be sorted then do it! So it may be that by Friday you have no petrol and that means you have to sort that before going to work, or it may be that you can never find any matching socks, or you can't find the kid's hair brush! You might be saying, goodness this is all very trivial, but think about it; often it is the trivial stuff that makes you blow your stack! So get rid of it, sort the things you can sort, do the sandwiches the night before, lay out the school uniforms when you put the kids to bed. You know what it is that causes the problems, and you know what you need to do to resolve the issues.

If you can sort out the easy things, then you will have more patience and time to deal with the bigger stuff that needs a bit more thinking space like how to dress a child in blue, white and red when their wardrobe only consists of green, black and yellow!!

See it's a piece of cake!

Lesson Twenty Three – Invest in YOU!

'My philosophy is whatever you do, you've got to invest in yourself. If you don't, there are a lot of people out there who will get the job because they're more prepared than you.'

Karl Urban

When I was unhappy, and I don't think that I was particularly untypical of unhappy people, the one person that I didn't invest in was me! I was more than happy to do anything for anybody else but I rarely did anything for me!

Now I'm not talking about ME time, which is a phrase that apparently the generation before us never had or talked about! I'm actually talking about investing in my physical and emotional me. Do you really look after yourself?

Think about a car – it needs a clean every now and then (just don't look at ours!) maybe a wax and polish, you need to get it serviced, MOT'd, change the oil, put petrol in it, look after the brakes etc. etc.

Compare this to yourself – do you really look after yourself?

Do you think about what you eat, drink, invest in a good hair cut (men a good shave!) – ladies do you grab the cheapest razor or do you go for a good wax?? Do you manicure, have a facial? Go for a massage or other therapy? Go for a run or a fitness class? When was the last time you added something to your wardrobe that wasn't in a sale??

I'm not saying that you have to do all of the above, go mad and spend oodles of money that you don't have. But it is important to question what you consider to be an investment – i.e what makes you feel good, what it is you do do, what you don't do, and why you don't do it!

If your answer is, well I can't justify spending that on myself, that would be £x over a year!......Think about it – who or what would you spend that money on? How would you feel if you did spend that money on yourself? If it is guilt – why are you feeling guilty? If the car needed £15 spent on it, would you spend it? Then why wouldn't you spend it on yourself? If you would feel better – then – well you have your answer!

The other issue is time. If you are saying you don't have time – then make time. We make time for important things and often for other people. You are not being selfish it is perfectly acceptable to give yourself some time, to recharge your batteries. If you find it hard – book it in your diary like you book in everybody else.

Some people might say, this is all very superficial. To be fair, it does depend on the person – what one person needs might not be what another needs, so it is important to ensure that we don't do things that we feel we 'should' do, but that we do things that we 'want' to do. Only we know what will make us feel better – if you find yourself saying I wish I could do……..that's usually a pretty good start.

We can go on, neglecting ourselves, but typically the member of the family that neglects themselves the most generally is the one that holds it all together – what happens if they can't function? If they break down like a car would? What use would they/you be then? And how much would you pay to put it right?

Lesson Twenty Four – Don't put off till tomorrow what you can do today!!!

'Procrastination makes easy things hard, hard things harder.'

Mason Cooley

This is probably something that your parents told you on a daily basis, and like me you didn't listen!

But stop for a moment and think about it, if there is something that you need to do, a phone call or a bill, maybe a letter or an email how does it feel when you don't do it straight away – or more importantly how does it feel when you **do** get it sorted straight away?

If you put something off, it lingers around like a black cloud getting bigger and bigger, heavier and heavier, often making it difficult for you to get on and do other things that you would much prefer to do – or if you do them you don't quite enjoy them as much as you would do had you done that **thing** which is hanging over you.

Eventually you will have to face and do whatever it is that you have been putting off and so it is just so much better to just get it out of the way and then you can get on with your life. Remember you deserve not to be stressed you deserve to be happy!

I find the best way to tackle such things is to make a list of all the things that I've been putting off, and give myself a time limit to get them done so that they don't take up all my time. It's a really good feeling when all those jobs you've been putting off are finally crossed off!

Another technique, is to tackle any jobs that arrive on bits of paper (like letters) is not to put the letter down until you have actioned it, otherwise you just find yourself picking the letter up and putting it down several times without actually doing anything! Quite often they don't actually take that long to do and you can get it out of the way immediately.

So really today's lesson is all about becoming a doer and not a procrastinator, make a list of all the things you have been putting off, choose at least two today and get them done (don't choose too many as you may become overwhelmed and not do any! Remember there is always tomorrow ;)).

Lesson Twenty Five – Make life interesting!

'Every night, I have to read a book, so that my mind will stop thinking about things that I stress about.'

Britney Spears

When was the last time you read a book for pleasure (other than this one)? A few years ago I asked myself the same question and I was shocked when I realised it had been a very long time since I had read a book for enjoyment and even longer since I had read a non-fiction book!

When we are at school we are constantly learning, picking up books that tell us so much about what is around us, but then we start the treadmill of life and we lose that motivation and opportunity to do so.

The first book I picked up at that time was about Queen Victoria and Haemophilia. I found it completely fascinating and I discovered that I could completely switch off from whatever was going on around me. Since then I've read hundreds of books ranging from all sorts of topics, both fiction and non-fiction (and even one written by my Husband!) It has become an interesting part of my life which takes me away from the everyday and gave me a richness that TV or social media doesn't.

So when was the last time you lost yourself in a book? When was the last time you learnt something new?

Just try it! You might be really surprised about the effect it might have!

Lesson Twenty Six – Focus on NOW!

'You practice mindfulness, on the one hand, to be calm and peaceful. On the other hand, as you practice mindfulness and live a life of peace, you inspire hope for a future of peace.'

Thich Nhat Hanh

When you were eating your breakfast this morning what were you thinking about?

What about when you were walking to school/driving/walking to work?

What about when you were eating your dinner?

The chances are you were thinking about something other than the thing that you were doing!

So often we are doing a simple thing like having a coffee but we are thinking about an issue at work/what to have for tea/how we are going to pay the mortgage or rent etc.

We sit there and instead of having a moment of calm, we are in a more stressed state worrying about what has been or what is about to come. This is human nature, but it is good to have a break from thinking about these things.

Trying to live in the present is a practice called mindfulness and like meditation it is used to quieten the mind and therefore the body.

But as a simple exercise, pick something that you do fairly regularly, like enjoying a latte or something similar, a time that you can be just quiet and enjoy that moment. Try not to think about anything else apart from what you are doing at that moment in time. If you struggle, if it is a drink or something to eat, think about how it tastes, or the texture etc. Look at your environment and focus on what is about you, what you can see and what you can hear. The object is to enjoy that moment and to remain in that moment – not in the past or in the future.

Lesson Twenty Seven – It's a natural thing!

'Autumn is a second spring when every leaf is a flower.'

Albert Camus

I find that nature is an incredibly calming and uplifting thing and it is all around us believe it or not!

Even in the busiest part of a city, you will find a lone butterfly, or flowers, a bee or a bird – there will be some element somewhere you just have to look for it. It often provides some beauty in an otherwise ugly environment.

My personal favourite are butterflies, just to watch them – look at how they are perfectly symmetrical. Observe how they fly and land, despite the busyness and chaos that is all around them, they just carry on regardless! Ants are great too – they are so busy, they remind me of our world sometimes, they are always rushing about looking like they are working so incredibly hard – especially when one is carrying something several times its own body weight!

For me as well, it is a reminder that nature is still there, we take it so much for granted and in many ways, we abuse and work against it, yet it still remains there for us. It acts as a real grounding mechanism, that there is this beautiful world around us that has just been provided – we don't really need to do anything to create it – it is just there.

One time on holiday I had hung a towel out and when it had dried a beautiful cricket was sunning itself on it. It was a most striking green made more so against the purple towel. The kids loved it as we could hear them but we had not seen one during our stay. Just for those few moments we were so fascinated by it – it was lovely.

So when you spot something, just think for a moment about how marvellous nature is, how it continues despite everything that we do.

Lesson Twenty Eight – Change your environment!

'We are what we see. We are products of our surroundings.'

Amber Valletta

This works well if you work from home as you have control over your space – but if you don't this works equally well with a space in your home that you spend a lot of time in.

How does it make you feel? Are you motivated? Calm? Happy? Uplifted? Or do you feel down? Unhappy? De-motivated?

This is a tricky one, as it may of course not be your surroundings at all that are causing these feelings, but if you find that you feel better in one room than in another, try to identify why you think that is? Often, but not always, we attach feelings to environments in the same way as we do to smells or music.

It may be that when you go into a room you sit in a particular chair and slump, you might feel like you can't be bothered anymore, you switch on the TV and before you know it you've been there an hour or so. However, when you walk into another room, you might sit and start motivating yourself as to how to spend your day – in ten minutes you are up and away.

You might sit in your home study and feel that you are not achieving anything. You look at your task list unsure where to start. You decide to get up and make a drink only to come back 15 minutes later feeling the same. Before you know it lunch time has come around and you've not achieved anything!

I find that if I am not feeling the emotion that I should feel in a particular room (e.g. motivated or calm) then it is time for a change. Sometimes as simple as moving the furniture about or moving some pictures, or even just sitting in a different spot just so that it looks different when I'm in there.

Sometimes it can be that it needs a good clear out and that there are things there that have been hanging around for a while – it's interesting how having clutter about can be quite de-motivating.

You will know what it is that is holding you back – whether it's where you sit, the pictures you are looking at, the colour of the walls, the surrounding 'stuff' – sometimes just shifting the furniture about will do the trick!

But I find that just changing some things about can really change the feel or energy of the room and have an effect on how I feel when I'm in there.

Lesson Twenty Nine – A gift from you....

'A friend is a gift you give yourself.'
Robert Louis Stevenson

When we get busy we often forget about the people who are closest to us. It may be a partner, a friend or a parent, but there is usually someone in our lives who means a lot to us and whom we rely on.

So today, do something for them. It may be that you are always appreciative of what they do but it is really that feeling of giving, of appreciating, and of them realising that you do appreciate everything that is the point of today's lesson.

It is such a lovely feeling when somebody does something for you, we can all buy a bunch of flowers or some chocolates from the local shop, but actually going out of our way to plan and organise something is really something quite special.

It might be breakfast in bed for our partner, it could be arranging a lunch or a tea, or even making something, it doesn't have to cost very much, it is more of a focus on you giving that person some of your time to say thank you to them.

And then when you've done it, reflect back on how you felt whilst you were doing it – you may well be surprised at just how uplifting it is!

Lesson Thirty – Wonder at the greatness of it all...

'For most people, we often marvel at the beauty of a sunrise or the magnificence of a full moon, but it is impossible to fathom the magnitude of the universe that surrounds us.'

Richard H. Baker

When was the last time you watched the sun rise, or set, or looked at the moon and the stars?

Often we get so caught up in the minutiae of life, the day to day, the mundane, the treadmill, that we lose sight of the big picture – of just how amazing this planet actually is.

So the next time there is a wonderful day, wait and watch the sun set, watch the colours as they reflect around the sky, the brightness, the enormity of it, the sheer beauty of it. Wake up early and watch a sun rise, look around at the world come alive after its night time sleep, listen to the birds wake each other with their dawn chorus, watch the sky as it slowly becomes bathed in light. (Please don't look directly at the sun though!)

If there is a clear night, go somewhere where it is out of the way of street lights (make sure you are safe!) and watch the sky. Watch and notice that the longer you look, the more stars you'll see, how some of the planets twinkle, what constellations can you see? Look at the moon – what shape is it what can you see on it, around it?

I find doing this so calming and because it is so fascinating, I think my favourite is going out on a full moon – there is something really magical about it – how it gives the world around you a different glow – there really isn't much to beat sitting out on a night under the stars with a firepit/burner and a glass of wine as you wonder about it all! And the best thing is that you rarely think about anything else whilst you are enjoying it!

Now You're Feeling Good in 30 Days!!

I hope you have enjoyed my ideas for reigniting that feel good factor. You may have worked through them one by one in order or chosen ones at random, it really doesn't matter because one of the things that I have learnt on this incredible journey is that you have to do what you feel is right for you! The fact that you have bought this book and read some of it is a big step in the right direction – you will be surprised at how you will notice other adjustments you can make or you may even create some of your own. I'd love to hear from you if you do – just email me

There are no right or wrong answers and if something doesn't work for you that's ok, this book was all about sharing my experience, not advising you what you must do, and I hope that it helps you open your mind to new ideas and new ways of doing things and hopefully find your feel good factor!

If you have enjoyed the book and you have some feel good thoughts that you would like to share or maybe you have created some of your own techniques, it would be great to hear from you. You can get hold of me in lots of different ways;

Twitter : https://twitter.com/EdenHsePublish

Website : http://www.edenhousepublishing.com/

e-mail : info@edenhousepublishing.com

Facebook: www.facebook.com/feelgoodfactorin30days

Coming soon…

More Feel Good Factor in 30 days!!

Don't miss your copy – register your interest at www.edenhousepublishing.com

Made in the USA
Charleston, SC
11 January 2014